PARTY TIME

and

THE NEW WORLD ORDER

PARTY TIME

and

THE NEW
WORLD ORDER

Two Plays by Harold Pinter

Grove Press
New York

Party Time was first published in Great Britain in 1991 by
Faber and Faber Limited.
The New World Order was first published in Great Britain
in 1993 by Faber and Faber Limited.
First Grove Press edition published in October 1993

Printed in the United States of America

FIRST EDITION

Library of Congress Cataloging-in-Publication Data
Pinter, Harold, 1930–
[Party Time]
Party time; and, The new world order: two plays / by
Harold Pinter—1st ed.
ISBN 0-8021-3352-5
I. Pinter, Harold, 1930– New world order. 1993.
II. Title.
III. Title: New world order.
PR6066.I53P37   1993   822'.914—dc20   93-28859

Grove Press
841 Broadway
New York, NY 10003

To Antonia

PARTY TIME

Party Time was first performed by the
Almeida Theatre Company on 31 October
1991 at the Almeida Theatre, London.
The cast was as follows:

TERRY	Peter Howitt
GAVIN	Barry Foster
DUSTY	Delia Roche
MELISSA	Dorothy Tutin
LIZ	Tacye Nichols
CHARLOTTE	Nicola Pagett
FRED	Roger Lloyd Pack
DOUGLAS	Gawn Grainger
JIMMY	Harry Burton
Director	Harold Pinter
Designer	Mark Thompson

Party Time was adapted by the author for television in 1992 and was transmitted on 17 November of that year. This is the version published here.

The play was performed by its original cast with the following additions:

SAM	Roland Oliver
PAMELA	Jill Johnson
EMILY	Julie-Christian Young
SUKI	Bridget Lynch Blosse
HARLOW	Kevin Dignam
SMITH	Ben Gray
WAITRESSES	Amelia Blacker and Rebecca Steele

The television production was produced by Michael Custance, designed by Grant Hicks and directed by Harold Pinter.

CHARACTERS

TERRY, a man of forty
GAVIN, a man in his fifties
DUSTY, a woman in her twenties
MELISSA, a woman of seventy
LIZ, a woman in her thirties
CHARLOTTE, a woman in her thirties
FRED, a man in his forties
DOUGLAS, a man of fifty
JIMMY, a young man

SAM, a man in his forties
PAMELA, a woman in her fifties
EMILY, a woman in her thirties
SUKI, a woman in her twenties
HARLOW, a man in his thirties
SMITH, a man in his twenties

1

Gavin's flat.

Sound of a distant helicopter.

People sitting, standing. WAITRESSES *with drinks trays. A bar.*

A large front door.

GAVIN *and* TERRY *standing with drinks.* HARLOW *and* SMITH *listening.*

TERRY

I tell you, it's got everything.

GAVIN

Has it?

TERRY

Oh, yes. Real class.

GAVIN

Really?

TERRY

Real class. I mean, what I mean to say, you play a game of tennis, you have a beautiful swim, they've got a bar right there –

Where?

TERRY

By the pool. You can have a fruit juice on the spot, no extra charge, then they give you this fantastic hot towel –

GAVIN

Hot?

TERRY

Wonderful. And I mean hot. I'm not joking.

GAVIN

Like the barber.

TERRY

Barber?

GAVIN

In the barber shop. When I was a boy.

TERRY

Oh yes?

Pause.

What do you mean?

GAVIN

They used to put a hot towel over your face,
you see, over your nose and eyes. I had it done
thousands of times. It got rid of all the
blackheads, all the blackheads on your face.

TERRY

Blackheads?

GAVIN

It burnt them out. The towels, you see, were
as hot as you could stand. That's what the
barber used to say: 'Hot enough for you, sir?'
It burnt all the blackheads out of your skin.

Pause.

I was born in the West Country, of course. So
I could be talking only of West Country
barber shops. But on the other hand I'm
pretty sure that hot towels for blackheads
were used in barber shops throughout the
land in those days. Yes, I believe it was
common practice in those days.

TERRY

Well, I'm sure it was. I'm sure it was. But no,
these towels I'm talking about are big bath
towels, towels for the body, I'm just talking
about pure comfort, that's why I'm telling
you, the place has got real class, it's got

everything. Mind you, there's a waiting list as long as – I mean you've got to be proposed and seconded, and then they've got to check you out, they don't let any old spare bugger in there, why should they?

GAVIN

Quite right.

TERRY

But of course it goes without saying that someone like yourself would be warmly welcome – as an honorary member.

GAVIN

How kind.

DUSTY *walks through the door and joins them.*

DUSTY

Did you hear what's happened to Jimmy? What's happened to Jimmy?

TERRY

Nothing's happened.

DUSTY

Nothing?

TERRY

Nobody is discussing this. Nobody's
discussing it, sweetie. Do you follow me?
Nothing's happened to Jimmy. And if you're
not a good girl I'll spank you.

DUSTY

What's going on?

TERRY

Tell him about the new club. I've just been
telling him about the club. She's a member.

GAVIN

What's it like?

DUSTY

Oh, it's beautiful. It's got everything. It's
beautiful. The lighting's wonderful. Isn't it?
Did you tell him about the alcoves?

TERRY

Well, there's a bar, you see, with glass
alcoves, looking out to under the water.

DUSTY

People swim at you, you see, while you're
having a drink.

TERRY

Lovely girls.

DUSTY

And men.

TERRY

Mostly girls.

DUSTY

Did you tell him about the food?

TERRY

The cannelloni is brilliant.

DUSTY

It's first class. The food is really first class.

TERRY

They even do chopped liver.

GAVIN

You couldn't describe that as a local dish.

MELISSA *comes through the door and joins them.*

MELISSA

What on earth's going on out there? It's like the Black Death.

TERRY

What is?

MELISSA

The town's dead. There's nobody on the
streets, there's not a soul in sight, apart from
some . . . soldiers. My driver had to stop at a
. . . you know . . . what do you call it? . . . a
roadblock. We had to say who we were . . . it
really was a trifle . . .

GAVIN

Oh, there's just been a little . . . you know . . .

TERRY

Nothing in it. Can I introduce you? Gavin
White – our host. Dame Melissa.

GAVIN

So glad you could come.

TERRY

What are you drinking?

A WAITRESS *approaches.*

Have a glass of champagne.

He hands MELISSA *a glass.*

DUSTY

I keep hearing all these things. I don't know
what to believe.

TERRY

What did you say?

DUSTY

I said I don't know what to believe.

TERRY

You don't have to believe anything. You just have to shut up and mind your own business, how many times do I have to tell you? You come to a lovely party like this, all you have to do is shut up and enjoy the hospitality and mind your own fucking business. How many more times do I have to tell you? You keep hearing all these things. You keep hearing all these things spread by pricks about pricks. What's it got to do with you?

GAVIN (*To* MELISSA)

Come and say hello . . .

He leads MELISSA *away.* TERRY *stares at* DUSTY.

2

SAM *and* PAMELA.

SAM

I say you've got to keep a sense of proportion.
You can't allow people to get things out of
proportion.

PAMELA

You mean you have to run a tight ship?

SAM

I think you do. Yes, I think you do. You see,
I've always been an absolutely straightforward man.

PAMELA

I can see that.

SAM

Really?

PAMELA

I can see it in your face. And in your stance.
You're straightforward. Quite right. We can't
afford to beat about the bush. We have to ask
direct questions. What is valuable? What is of
value? That is my question. What are the
values we choose to protect and why?

Quite.

Quite what?

No, no – I mean – well, yes . . . exactly . . .

3

LIZ *and* CHARLOTTE.

LIZ

So beautiful. The mouth, really. And of
course the eyes.

CHARLOTTE

Yes.

LIZ

Not to mention his hands. I'll tell you, I
would have killed –

CHARLOTTE

I could see –

LIZ

But that bitch had her legs all over him.

CHARLOTTE

I know.

LIZ

I thought she was going to crush him to death.

CHARLOTTE

Unbelievable.

LIZ

Her skirt was right up to her neck – did you see?

CHARLOTTE

So barefaced –

LIZ

Next minute she's lugging him up the stairs.

CHARLOTTE

I saw.

LIZ

But as he was going, do you know what he did?

CHARLOTTE

What?

LIZ

He looked at me.

CHARLOTTE

Did he?

LIZ

I swear it. As he was being lugged out he
looked back, he looked back, I swear, at me,
like a wounded deer, I shall never, as long as I
live, forget it, I shall never forget that look.

CHARLOTTE

How beautiful.

LIZ

I could have cut her throat, that
nymphomaniac slut.

CHARLOTTE

Yes, but think what happened. Think of the
wonderful side of it. Because for you it was
love, it was falling in love. That's what it was,
wasn't it? You fell in love.

LIZ

I did. You're right. I fell in love. I am in love. I
haven't slept all night. I'm in love.

CHARLOTTE

How many times does that happen? That's
the point. How often does it really happen?
How often does anyone experience such a
thing?

LIZ

Yes, you're right. That's what happened to
me. That is what has happened – to me.

CHARLOTTE

That's why you're in such pain.

LIZ

Yes, because that bigtitted tart –

CHARLOTTE

Raped the man you love.

LIZ

Yes she did. That's what she did. She raped
my beloved.

4

FRED *and* DOUGLAS.

FRED

We've got to make it work.

DOUGLAS

What?

FRED

The country.

Pause.

DOUGLAS

You've brought the house down with that one, Fred.

FRED

But that's what matters. That's what matters. Doesn't it?

DOUGLAS

Oh, it matters. It matters. I should say it matters. All this fucking-about has to stop.

FRED

You mean it?

DOUGLAS

I mean it all right.

FRED

I admire people like you.

DOUGLAS

So do I.

FRED *clenches his fist.*

FRED

A bit of that.

DOUGLAS *clenches his fist.*

DOUGLAS
A bit of that.

5

EMILY *and* SUKI.

EMILY
We're going to Sorley next weekend for the Horse Trials. The children love it.

SUKI
Is your husband jumping?

EMILY
Well, it's actually the horse that jumps. My husband is competing.

SUKI
I've watched him jump. He's awfully good.

EMILY *looks at her.*

Well, you know what I mean –

EMILY
You've watched him? Where?

SUKI

Oh, somewhere up north, I think.

EMILY

I'm sure the boys are going to follow in his footsteps. They worship their father.

SUKI

He's not coming here tonight then?

EMILY

Well, of course he's not. He's busy. (*She points to the window.*) Down there.

SUKI

Oh, of course.

6

FRED *and* DOUGLAS.

FRED

How's it going tonight?

DOUGLAS

Like clockwork. Look. Let me tell you something. We want peace. We want peace and we're going to get it.

FRED

Quite right.

DOUGLAS

We want peace and we're going to get it. But
we want that peace to be cast iron. No leaks.
No draughts. Cast iron. Tight as a drum. That's
the kind of peace we want and that's the kind
of peace we're going to get. A cast-iron peace.

He clenches his fist.

Like this.

FRED

You know, I really admire people like you.

DOUGLAS

So do I.

*They move away. The camera stays looking at
the closed front door.*

7

HARLOW, SMITH *and* PAMELA.

HARLOW

Mike Harlow.

SMITH

Simon Smith. Assistants to Mr White.

PAMELA

You're Cynthia Harlow's boy.

HARLOW

I am, yes.

PAMELA

We were at Oxford together. Does she still
love dogs?

HARLOW

Dogs are her life.

PAMELA

At Oxford she was fully expected to marry a
dog.

She studies HARLOW.

She apparently didn't.

8

MELISSA, DUSTY, TERRY *and* GAVIN.

MELISSA (*To* DUSTY)

How sweet of you to say so.

DUSTY

But you do have a really wonderful figure.
Honestly. Doesn't she?

TERRY

I've known this lady for years. Haven't I?
How many years have I known you? Years.
And she's always looked the same. Haven't
you? She's always looked the same. Hasn't
she?

GAVIN

Has she?

DUSTY

Always. Haven't you?

TERRY

She has. Isn't that right?

MELISSA

Oh, you're joking.

TERRY

Not me. I never joke. Have you ever heard me
crack a joke?

MELISSA

No, if I still look all right, it's probably because I've just joined this new club – (*To* GAVIN) Do you know it?

TERRY

We were just telling him. We were just telling him all about it.

MELISSA

Oh, were you?

GAVIN

Just now, yes. Sounds delightful. You're a member, are you?

MELISSA

Oh yes. I think it's saved my life. The swimming. Why don't you join? Do you play tennis?

GAVIN

I'm a golfer. I play golf.

MELISSA

What else do you do?

GAVIN (*Smiling*)

I don't understand what you mean.

TERRY

What else does he do? He doesn't do anything
else. He plays golf. That's what he does.
That's all he does. He plays golf.

GAVIN

Well . . . I do sail. I do own a boat.

DUSTY

I love boats.

TERRY

What?

DUSTY

I love boats. I love boating.

TERRY

Boating. Did you hear that?

DUSTY

I love cooking on boats.

TERRY

The only thing she doesn't like on boats is
being fucked on boats. That's what she
doesn't like.

MELISSA

That's funny. I thought everyone liked that.

GAVIN *and* TERRY *laugh.*

DUSTY

Does anyone know what's happened to my
brother Jimmy?

TERRY

I don't know what it is. Perhaps she's deaf or
perhaps my voice isn't strong enough or
distinct enough. What do you think, folks?
Perhaps there's something faulty with my
diction. I'm forced to float all these
possibilities because I thought I had said that
we don't discuss this question of what has
happened to Jimmy, that it's not up for
discussion, that it's not on anyone's agenda. I
thought I had already made that point quite
clearly. But perhaps my voice isn't strong
enough or perhaps my articulation isn't good
enough or perhaps she's deaf.

DUSTY

It's on my agenda.

TERRY

What did you say?

DUSTY

I said it's on my agenda.

TERRY

No no, you've got it wrong there, old darling.
What you've got wrong there, old darling,
what you've got totally wrong, is that you
don't have any agenda. Got it? You have no
agenda. Absolutely the opposite is the case.
(*To the others*) I'm going to have to give her a
real talking to when I get her home, I can see
that.

GAVIN

So odd, the number of men who can't control
their wives.

TERRY

What?

GAVIN (*To* MELISSA)

It's the root of so many ills, you know.
Uncontrollable wives.

MELISSA

Yes, I know what you mean.

TERRY

What are you saying to me?

GAVIN (*To* MELISSA)

I went for a walk in the woods the other day. I
had no idea how many squirrels were still left
in this country. I find them such vivacious

creatures, quite enchanting.

I used to love them as a girl.

GAVIN
Did you really? What about hawks?

MELISSA
Oh I loved hawks too. And eagles. But
certainly hawks. The kestrel. The way it flew,
and hovered, over my valley. It made me cry. I
still cry.

9

*The front door is ajar. The light through it
gradually intensifies. It burns into the room.*

Silhouetted figures moving in foreground.

10

DOUGLAS, FRED, LIZ *and* CHARLOTTE.

DOUGLAS
Oh, have you met my wife?

FRED (*To* LIZ)

How do you do?

LIZ

This is Charlotte.

FRED

We've met before.

LIZ

You've met before?

CHARLOTTE

Oh yes. We've met. He gave me a leg up in life.

DOUGLAS

Did you really? How exciting.

FRED

It was.

DOUGLAS

Was it exciting for you too? To be given a leg up?

CHARLOTTE

Mmmmnnn. Yes. Oh, yes. I'm still trembling.

DOUGLAS

How exciting.

I think this is such a gorgeous party. Don't
you? I mean I just think it's such a gorgeous
party. Don't you? I think it's such fun. I love
the fact that people are so well dressed.
Casual but good. Do you know what I mean?
Is it silly to say I feel proud? I mean to be part
of the society of beautifully dressed people?
Oh, God I don't know, elegance, style, grace,
taste, don't these words, these concepts, mean
anything any more? I'm not alone, am I, in
thinking them incredibly important? Anyway
I love everything that flows. I can't tell you
how happy I feel.

FRED (*To* CHARLOTTE)
You married someone. I've forgotten who it
was.

Long silence.

CHARLOTTE
He died.

Silence.

DOUGLAS
If you're free this summer do come to our
island. We take an island for the summer. Do
come. There's more or less nobody there. Just
a few local people who do us proud. Terribly

civil. Everything works. I have my own generator. But the storms are wild, aren't they darling? If you like storms. Siroccos. Makes you feel alive. Truly alive. Makes the old pulse go rat-at-at-tat. God it can be wild, can't it darling? Makes the old pulse go rat-at-at-tat. Raises the ante. You know. Gets the blood up. Actually, when I'm out there on the island I feel ten years younger. I could take anyone on. Man, woman or child, what?

He laughs.

I could take a wild animal on. But then when the storm is over and night falls and the moon is out in all its glory and all you're left with is the rhythm of the sea, of the waves, you know what God intended for the human race, you know what paradise is.

11

SAM, HARLOW *and* SMITH.

SAM
What is right is right, that's what I say.

HARLOW
Exactly.

SAM

I mean, if a thing works, if a thing is right, respect that, acknowledge it, respect it and hold to it.

SMITH

Hold on to it.

SAM

Hold *to* it. We're talking about principles. I mean, I met a man at a party the other day – I couldn't believe it – He was talking the most absolute bloody crap – his ideas about the world, that kind of thing – he was a complete and utter and total arsehole – a musician or something –

SMITH

Stoddart?

SAM

That's it. Now, you see, these kind of people, they're an infection.

SMITH

Don't worry about Stoddart. We've seen him off.

HARLOW

We've had him for breakfast.

SMITH *and* HARLOW *laugh.*

12

TERRY *and* DUSTY.

TERRY
Are you mad? Do you know what that man
is?

DUSTY
Yes, I think I know what that man is.

TERRY
You don't know what he is. You have no
idea. You don't know what his position is.
You have simply no idea. You simply have no
idea.

DUSTY
He has lovely manners. He seems to come
from another world. A courteous, caring
world. He'll send me flowers in the morning.

TERRY
No he bloody won't. Oh no he bloody won't.

DUSTY
Poor darling, are you upset? Have I let you

down? I've let you down. And I've always tried to be such a good wife. Such a good wife.

They stare at each other.

Perhaps you'll kill me when we get home? Do you think you will? Do you think you'll put an end to it? Do you think there is an end to it? What do you think? Do you think that if you put an end to me that would be the end of everything for everyone? Will everything and everyone die with me?

TERRY

Yes, you're all going to die together, you and all your lot.

DUSTY

How are you going to do it? Tell me.

TERRY

Easy. We've got dozens of options. We could suffocate every single one of you at a given signal or we could shove a broomstick up each individual arse at another given signal or we could poison all the mother's milk in the world so that every baby would drop dead before it opened its perverted bloody mouth.

DUSTY

But will it be fun for me? Will it be fun?

TERRY

You'll love it. But I'm not going to tell you
which method we'll use. I just want you to
have a lot of sexual anticipation. I want you
to look forward to whatever the means
employed with a lot of sexual anticipation.

DUSTY

But you still love me?

TERRY

Of course I love you. You're the mother of my
children.

DUSTY

Oh incidentally, what's happened to Jimmy?

13

PAMELA, EMILY *and* SUKI.

PAMELA

Oh, I used to play, yes, as a girl. Loved it. My
father was a marvellous player. A great
smasher at the net.

SUKI

Do you know Robert Cowley? Emily's
husband? The showjumper?

PAMELA

I don't in fact *know* him, but –

SUKI

He's a wonderful tennis player. (*To* EMILY)
Isn't he?

EMILY

He's top of the ladder at the club.

PAMELA

Ladder?

EMILY

Yes, the tennis ladder at the club – you know
– our club – he's top of the ladder.

SUKI

Swingeing forehand. Literally swingeing.

EMILY

Well, actually he is in fact a totally
accomplished all-round athlete.

SUKI

Doesn't he jump for the army?

EMILY *stares at her.*

          PAMELA (*To* EMILY)
You must be so proud.

14

FRED *and* CHARLOTTE.

          FRED
Such a long time.

          CHARLOTTE
Such a long time.

          FRED
Isn't it?

          CHARLOTTE
Oh, yes. Ages.

          FRED
You're looking as beautiful as ever.

          CHARLOTTE
So are you.

          FRED
Me? Not me.

CHARLOTTE

Oh, you are. Well, in a manner of speaking.

FRED

What do you mean, in a manner of speaking?

CHARLOTTE

Oh, I meant you look as beautiful as ever.

FRED

But I never was beautiful. In any way.

CHARLOTTE

No, that's true. You weren't. In any way at all. I've been talking shit. In a manner of speaking.

FRED

Your language was always deplorable.

CHARLOTTE

Yes. Appalling.

FRED

Are you enjoying the party?

CHARLOTTE

Best party I've been to in years.

Pause.

FRED

You said your husband died.

CHARLOTTE

My what?

FRED

Your husband.

CHARLOTTE

Oh my husband. Oh yes. That's right. He died.

FRED

Was it a long illness?

CHARLOTTE

Short.

FRED

Ah.

Pause.

Quick then.

CHARLOTTE

Quick, yes. Short and quick.

Pause.

Better that way.

CHARLOTTE

Really?

FRED

I would have thought.

CHARLOTTE

Ah. I see. Yes.

Pause.

Better for who?

FRED

What?

CHARLOTTE

You said it would be better. Better for who?

FRED

For you.

CHARLOTTE *laughs.*

CHARLOTTE

Yes! I'm glad you didn't say him.

FRED

Well, I could say him. A quick death must be better than a slow one. It stands to reason.

CHARLOTTE

No it doesn't.

Pause.

Anyway, I'll bet it can be quick and slow at the same time. I bet it can. I bet death can be both things at the same time. Oh by the way, he wasn't ill.

Pause.

FRED

You're still very beautiful.

CHARLOTTE

I think there's something going on in the street.

FRED

What?

CHARLOTTE

I think there's something going on in the street.

FRED

Leave the street to us.

CHARLOTTE

Who's us?

FRED

Oh, just us . . . you know.

She stares at him.

CHARLOTTE

God, your looks! No, seriously. You're still so handsome! How do you do it? What's your diet? What's your regime? What *is* your regime by the way? What do you do to keep yourself so . . . I don't know . . . so . . . oh, I don't know . . . so trim, so fit?

FRED

I lead a clean life.

DOUGLAS *and* LIZ *join them.*

CHARLOTTE (*To* DOUGLAS)

Do you too?

DOUGLAS

Do I what?

CHARLOTTE

Fred says he looks so fit and so . . . handsome
. . . because he leads a clean life. What about
you?

DOUGLAS

I lead an incredibly clean life. It doesn't make
me handsome but it makes me happy.

LIZ

And it makes me happy too. So happy.

DOUGLAS

Even though I'm not handsome?

LIZ

But you are. You are. Isn't he? He is. You are.
Isn't he?

DOUGLAS *puts his arm around her.*

DOUGLAS

When we were first married we lived in a
two-roomed flat. I was – I'll be frank – I was a
traveller, a commercial traveller, a salesman –
it's true, that's what I was and I don't deny it
– and travel I did. Didn't I? Travel I did.
Because my little girl here had given birth to
twins.

He laughs.

Can you believe it? Twins. I had to slave my guts out, I can tell you. But this girl here, this little girl here, do you know what she did? She looked after those twins all by herself! No maid, no help, nothing. She did it herself – all by herself. And when I got back from my travelling I would find the flat immaculate, the twins bathed and in bed, tucked up in bed, fast asleep, my wife looking beautiful and my dinner in the oven.

FRED *applauds*.

And that's why we're still together.

He kisses LIZ *on the cheek*.

That's why we're still together.

15

HARLOW *and* SMITH *walk through the empty hall. The front door is closed. They stop, look down the corridors and then go out of shot. The camera follows them, then slowly pans back to the front door. It is now ajar. The light through it gradually intensifies. It burns into the room.*

16

TERRY, DUSTY, GAVIN, MELISSA, FRED,
CHARLOTTE, DOUGLAS, LIZ, SAM, PAMELA,
EMILY, SUKI, HARLOW *and* SMITH.

TERRY

The thing is, it is actually real value for money.
Now this is a very, very unusual thing. It is an
extremely unusual thing these days to find that
you are getting real value for money. You take
your hand out of your pocket and you put your
money down and you know what you're
getting. And what you're getting is absolutely
gold-plated service. Gold-plated service in all
departments. You've got real catering. You've
got catering on all levels. You've not only got
very good catering in itself – you know, food,
that kind of thing – and napkins – you know,
all that, wonderful, first rate – but you've also
got artistic catering – you actually have an
atmosphere – in this club – which is catering
artistically for its clientele. I'm referring to the
kind of light, the kind of paint, the kind of
music, the club offers. I'm talking about a truly
warm and harmonious environment. You
won't find voices raised in our club. People
don't do vulgar and sordid and offensive
things. And if they do we kick them in the balls
and chuck them down the stairs with no
trouble at all.

Can I subscribe to all that has just been said?

Pause.

I would like to subscribe to all that has just
been said. I would like to add my voice. I have
belonged to many tennis and swimming clubs.
Many tennis and swimming clubs. And at
some of these clubs I first met some of my
dearest friends. All of them are now dead.
Every friend I ever had. Or ever met. Is dead.
They are all of them dead. Every single one of
them. I have absolutely not one left. None are
left. Nothing is left. What was it all for? The
tennis and the swimming clubs? What was it
all for? What?

Silence.

But the clubs died too and rightly so. I mean
there is a distinction to be made. My friends
went the way of all flesh and I don't regret
their passing. They weren't my friends
anyway. I couldn't stand half of them. But the
clubs! The clubs died, the swimming and the
tennis clubs died because they were based on
ideas which had no moral foundation, no
moral foundation whatsoever. But *our* club,
our club – is a club which is activated, which
is inspired by a moral sense, a moral

awareness, a set of moral values which is – I
have to say – unshakeable, rigorous,
fundamental, constant. Thank you.

Applause.

17

Phone ringing. HARLOW *picks it up.*

HARLOW
Yes? . . . Thank you.

He puts the phone down.

18

The group.

GAVIN
Yes, I'm terribly glad you've said all that.

HARLOW *approaches* GAVIN *and whispers in
his ear.* GAVIN *nods and turns to the others.*

Aren't you?

DOUGLAS

First rate.

LIZ

So moving.

PAMELA

Absolutely right!

TERRY

Fantastic.

EMILY

Lovely!

FRED

Right on the nail.

SUKI

Spot on!

CHARLOTTE

So true.

SMITH

Great.

DUSTY

Oh yes.

She claps her hands.

Oh yes.

SAM

Terrific.

DOUGLAS

Absolutely first rate.

GAVIN

Yes, it was first rate. And it desperately
needed saying. And how splendid that it was
said tonight, at such an enjoyable party, in
such congenial company. I must say I speak as
a very happy host. And by the way, I'll really
have to join this wonderful club of yours,
won't I?

TERRY

You're elected forthwith. You're an honorary
member. As of today.

Laughter and applause.

GAVIN

Thank you very much indeed. Now I believe
one or two of our guests encountered traffic
problems on their way here tonight. I
apologize for that, but I would like to assure
you that all such problems and all related
problems will be resolved very soon. Between
ourselves, we've had a bit of a round-up this

evening. This round-up is coming to an end. In fact normal services will be resumed shortly. That is, after all, our aim. Normal service. We, if you like, insist on it. We will insist on it. We do. That's all we ask, that the service this country provides will run on normal, secure and legitimate paths and that the ordinary citizen be allowed to pursue his labours and his leisure in peace. Thank you all so much for coming here tonight. It's been really lovely to see you, quite smashing.

WAITRESSES *enter with champagne. Laughter. A tumult of voices.*

19

Laughter continuing. Shifting bodies. At the very far end of the hall the front door can be seen. It is wide open. The light burns into the room. A young man stands in the frame of the door. He is thinly dressed.

The camera moves through the crowd towards him. The sounds die.

JIMMY
Sometimes I hear things. Then it's quiet.

I had a name. It was Jimmy. People called me Jimmy. That was my name.

Sometimes I hear things. Then everything is quiet. When everything is quiet I hear my heart. When the terrible noises come I don't hear anything. Don't hear don't breathe am blind.

Then everything is quiet. I hear a heartbeat. It is probably not my heartbeat. It is probably someone else's heartbeat.

What am I?

Sometimes a door bangs, I hear voices, then it stops. Everything stops. It all stops. It all closes. It closes down. It shuts. It all shuts. It shuts down. It shuts. I see nothing at any time any more. I sit sucking the dark.

It's what I have. The dark is in my mouth and I suck it. It's the only thing I have. It's mine. It's my own. I suck it.

THE NEW WORLD ORDER

The New World Order was first performed
on 19 July 1991 at the Royal Court Theatre
Upstairs, London. The cast was as follows:

DES	Bill Paterson
LIONEL	Michael Byrne
BLINDFOLDED MAN	Douglas McFerran
Director	Harold Pinter
Designer	Ian MacNeil
Lighting	Kevin Sleep

A blindfolded man sitting on a chair.
*Two men (*DES *and* LIONEL*) looking at him.*

DES

Do you want to know something about this
man?

LIONEL

What?

DES

He hasn't got any idea at all of what we're
going to do to him.

LIONEL

He hasn't, no.

DES

He hasn't, no. He hasn't got any idea at all
about any one of the number of things that we
might do to him.

LIONEL

That we will do to him.

DES

That we will.

Pause.

Well, some of them. We'll do some of them.

LIONEL

Sometimes we do all of them.

DES

That can be counterproductive.

LIONEL

Bollocks.

They study the man. He is still.

DES

But anyway here he is, here he is sitting here,
and he hasn't the faintest idea of what we
might do to him.

LIONEL

Well, he probably has the *faintest* idea.

DES

A faint idea, yes. Possibly.

DES *bends over the man.*

Have you? What do you say?

He straightens.

Let's put it this way. He has *little* idea of what
we might do to him, of what in fact we are
about to do to him.

LIONEL

Or his wife. Don't forget his wife. He has little idea of what we're about to do to his wife.

DES

Well, he probably has *some* idea, he's probably got *some* idea. After all, he's read the papers.

LIONEL

What papers?

Pause.

DES

You're right there.

LIONEL

Who is this cunt anyway? What is he, some kind of peasant – or a lecturer in theology?

DES

He's a lecturer in fucking peasant theology.

LIONEL

Is he? What about his wife?

DES

Women don't have theological inclinations.

LIONEL

Oh, I don't know. I used to discuss that
question with my mother – quite often.

DES

What question?

LIONEL

Oh you know, the theological aspirations of
the female.

Pause.

DES

What did she say?

LIONEL

She said . . .

DES

What?

Pause.

LIONEL

I can't remember.

He turns to the man in the chair.

Motherfucker.

DES

Fuckpig.

They walk round the chair.

LIONEL

You know what I find really disappointing?

DES

What?

LIONEL

The level of ignorance that surrounds us.
I mean, this prick here –

DES

You called him a cunt last time.

LIONEL

What?

DES

You called him a cunt last time. Now you call
him a prick. How many times do I have to tell
you? You've got to learn to define your terms
and stick to them. You can't call him a cunt in
one breath and a prick in the next. The terms
are mutually contradictory. You'd lose face in
any linguistic discussion group, take my tip.

LIONEL

Christ. Would I?

DES

Definitely. And you know what it means to
you. You know what language means to you.

LIONEL

Yes, I do know.

DES

Yes, you do know. Look at this man here, for
example. He's a first class example. See what I
mean? Before he came in here he was a big
shot, he never stopped shooting his mouth
off, he never stopped questioning received
ideas. Now – because he's apprehensive about
what's about to happen to him – he's stopped
all that, he's got nothing more to say, he's
more or less called it a day. I mean once – not
too long ago – this man was a man of
conviction, wasn't he, a man of principle.
Now he's just a prick.

LIONEL

Or a cunt.

DES

And we haven't even finished with him. We
haven't begun.

LIONEL

No, we haven't even finished with him. We haven't even finished with him! Well, we haven't begun.

DES

And there's still his wife to come.

LIONEL

That's right. We haven't finished with him. We haven't even begun. And we haven't finished with his wife either.

DES

We haven't even begun.

LIONEL *puts his hand over his face and sobs.*

DES

What are you crying about?

LIONEL

I love it. I love it. I love it.

He grasps DES's *shoulder.*

Look. I have to tell you. I've got to tell you. There's no one else I can tell.

DES

All right. Fine. Go on. What is it? Tell me.

Pause.

                    LIONEL
I feel so pure.

Pause.

                    DES
Well, you're right. You're right to feel pure.
You know why?

                    LIONEL
Why?

                    DES
Because you're keeping the world clean for
democracy.

They look into each other's eyes.

                    DES
I'm going to shake you by the hand.

DES *shakes* LIONEL's *hand. He then gestures
to the man in the chair with his thumb.*

And so will he . . . (*he looks at his watch*) . . .
in about thirty-five minutes.